RATS
A Quarterly

Daniel R. Schwartz, M.S., D.V.M.

Photography: Michael Gilroy, Nick Mays, Daniel R. Schwartz

ABOUT QUARTERLIES

T.F.H. quarterlies are published in both magazine format and normal book format, at different prices of course. The concept behind this type of publishing is getting the information to you as quickly and reasonably priced as possible. Magazine formats are accustomed to being produced in 30 days; books have almost no time limit. Thus our Quarterlies are published by our magazine staff.

ABOUT THE AUTHOR

Dr. Daniel R. Schwartz is a board-certified specialist in laboratory animal medicine. Dr. Schwartz has worked in small animal practice, in academic and medical centers, and in industry caring for companion, zoo, and laboratory animals. Dr. Schwartz decided to write this text after contacting T.F.H. Publications about using Nylabone® products to enrich the cage environment of laboratory rats.

CONTENTS

Introduction 2
The Rat as a Companion Animal 3
Origin & Development 4
External Anatomy & General Physiology 8
Acquiring a Rat 15
Husbandry 16
Handling 22
Nutrition 24
Behavior & Training 27
Reproduction 30
Diseases 36
Sources of Additional Information/Clubs 47
Index 48

DEDICATION

This publication is dedicated to those rats used in research and to the people who care for them. Hence, all the author's proceeds have been donated to the American Association of Laboratory Animal Science, formerly known as the Animal Care Panel.

yearBOOKS, INC.

Dr. Herbert R. Axelrod,
   Founder & Chairman
Neal Pronek
   Chief Editor

yearBOOKS are all photo composed, color separated, and designed on Scitex equipment in Neptune, N.J. with the following staff:

DIGITAL PRE-PRESS
   Robert Onyrscuk
   Jose Reyes
   Michael L. Secord

COMPUTER ART
   Sherise Buhagiar
   Patti Escabi
   Sandra Taylor Gale
   Pat Marotta
   Candida Moreira
   Joanne Muzyka

Advertising Sales
George Campbell
   Chief
Amy Manning
   Director

©yearBOOKS,Inc.
1 TFH Plaza
Neptune, N.J. 07753
Completely manufactured in Neptune, N.J.
USA

INTRODUCTION

Rats: A Quarterly is written for the pet rat owner. Therefore, the purpose is to provide practical and accurate information on the general biology, care, behavior, reproduction, and health of rats as pets or companion animals.

Much is known about rats, as rats are second only to mice in usage in research. Each year millions of rats are used as research animals; much fewer are kept as pets. Accordingly, there are many books about rats as research animals and few books about rats as pets. The large data base of information on the care of research rats is placed in the field of laboratory animal science.

Research animals are cared for by professionals who are trained in laboratory animal science and medicine. Good animal care is essential to accomplish good research. Genetics, nutrition, stress, and disease are all known to affect experiments. Therefore, research animals must be given the best care since they are the foundation of many expensive research projects. In addition, governments, regulatory agencies, and organizations have regulations and guidelines ensuring the humane care and valid use of animals in research and teaching.

Many of the principles of laboratory animal science apply as well to companion animals. Good animal care is also essential to the health and well-being of companion

A five-month-old black-hooded female rat. Hooded rats are spotted rats with pigmented fur on the head and shoulders, that is, the "hood," and an irregular stripe down the back. The unique pattern of blotches can serve to identify an individual hooded rat.

animals. Serious owners of "unusual" pets can often find excellent information in texts on laboratory animal science and medicine, as many species of animals are studied by scientists. Of course, in the case of rats, this is especially true. Differing from this book, laboratory animal science texts usually have additional sections on internal anatomy, dosing procedures, specimen collection, drugs and anesthesia.

Unlike the situation for most hobbyists, at most research facilities, the production and care of rats are on a grand scale. Good animal research facilities utilize analyzed feed,

bedding and water, filtered room air with monitored air changes, tightly controlled room temperature and humidity levels, automatic lighting, and rigid sanitation procedures.

Some of the illustrations and interpretations presented here do reflect the optimal conditions and equipment found in most research facilities. For example, the wearing of gloves when handling animals to minimize the possibility of spreading disease from animal to animal or between animal and people. The conditions for caring for pet rats are much more relaxed.

THE RAT AS A COMPANION ANIMAL

Rats make great pets. Because of their small size, they sometimes are referred to as pocket pets. Rats are inexpensive. They are simple to house, feed, breed, and train. Rats have the intelligence to be able to recognize you and to remember events and places. Your rat will develop its own unique personality with its own likes and dislikes. Over its modest life span of two to three years, your pet rat will develop a feeling of dependency on your care, which in turn will foster a mutually beneficial human/animal bond between you and your pet.

REPUTATION

In Western cultures, many people have superstitions about rats as being bad or evil. Rats have been called the "devil's lapdogs" and have been associated with witches and sorcery in fictitious literature. Horror movies like *Willard* (1971) and *Ben* (1972) have not improved the rat's reputation.

In some Eastern cultures, rats are held in higher esteem. The Chinese zodiac or calendar has a "year of the rat." People born in that year are said to be imaginative, charming, and generous, although also quick-tempered, overly critical and somewhat aggressive and opportunistic.

Much of the fear of rats is attributed to the wild rat's reputation for aggressiveness and spreading diseases. Through domestication, the pet rat's behavior may be as different from its wild cousins as is the dog's to the wolf's. Pet rats should be obtained from "clean" sources; and thus, they should pose no disease hazard to people. In fact, they may be safer pets than some of the more common companion animals.

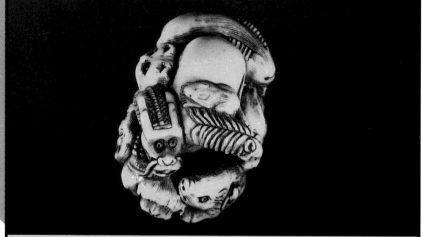

This netsuke (a small, intricately carved toggle) depicts all of the 12 animals that represent the years in the Chinese zodiac. People born under the sign of the rat (that is, born in the years 1924, 1936, 1948, 1960, 1972, 1984, 1996...) are said to be successful as writers, critics, and publicists. Some famous people born under the sign of the rat: Mozart, Winston Churchill, George Washington, and Truman Capote.

Rats are popular pets because they are intelligent, interesting, and easy to care for.

ORIGIN & DEVELOPMENT

SCIENTIFIC CLASSIFICATION

Pet, or fancy, rats are domesticated varieties of the Norway, or brown, rat, *Rattus norvegicus*, a species in the family Muridae in the order Rodentia. Adult wild Norway rats weigh from 200 to 485 grams, are 12 to 18 inches long, have tails shorter than the combined lengths of the head and body, typically have a brown agouti coat and a tan underbelly, have a body with a round abdomen, a head with a short muzzle, and thick ears shorter than $3/4$ of an inch and covered with fine hair. They are noted for burrowing and aggressive behaviors.

There are many other animals also called rats. The genus *Rattus* includes over 100 species. The family Muridae has over 100 genera as does the family Cricetidae, which also has many species commonly referred to as rats. Most of these other rats are not suitable as pets, as they do not adapt well to living and breeding in captivity. Of the rats, the Norway rat and the black rat, *Rattus rattus*, are the two species that have had the greatest impact on human civilization.

The black rat is also called the roof, house, ship, or Alexandrine rat. Adult black rats weigh from 115 to 350 grams, are 12 to 18 inches long, have tails longer than the combined lengths of the head and body, typically have a dusky black or gray coat and a lighter underbelly, have a body with a slender abdomen, a head with a long muzzle, ears longer than $3/4$ of an inch and not covered with hair, and are noted for climbing ability and nesting above the ground. Black rats are often displaced by the larger, more aggressive Norway rat when the two rats are in the same environment. There are no laboratory or domestic strains of *Rattus rattus*.

ORIGIN AND SPREAD

Rats are native to the region of Asia, including Asia Minor to India. Through introduction by humans, they are now found nearly worldwide. If judged by population spread and size, your pet rat is a member of one of the most successful groups of mammals to have orbited the earth.

The black rat reached Europe around the twelfth century by means of trade and military routes. The black rat is the rat associated with the Black Death, the bubonic plague of the fourteenth century. From the fourteenth to eighteenth centuries, bubonic plagues killed 25 million Europeans. The disease is caused by the bacterium *Yersinia pestis*, which can be transmitted directly from infected rodents to people or indirectly by rat fleas. From Europe, the black rat arrived in America in the sixteenth century as stowaways on ships.

The Norway rat's migration followed that of the wild black rat and reached Europe from Asia by the early eighteenth century. There is no scientific reason for these rats to be

A young Siamese male rat. For many rat fanciers, the development of new color varieties is one of the most challenging aspects of the hobby.

This domestic female agouti rat has the typical brown agouti coat and tan underbelly of its wild relative, the Norway, or brown, rat, Rattus norvegicus.

named with reference to Norway, as they did not originate or specifically spread from this country. Wild Norway rats reached North America around 1775.

While the wild Norway rat and the black rat have benefited with shelter and food by living in close proximity to humans, humans have suffered greatly. Besides plague, wild rats have carried such diseases as murine typhus, salmonellosis, rat-bite fever, tularemia, trichinosis, and leptospirosis. Together with the house mouse, *Mus musculus*, rats are responsible for consuming or spoiling approximately one-fifth of the world's crops each year. Structural damage, floods, and fires have resulted from rats gnawing and burrowing.

The destruction and disease caused by wild rats can be said to be somewhat offset by the animal research that has resulted in the improvement in the health of both people and animals. Over 90% of all laboratory animals are rodents; and, laboratory rats account for approximately 20-25% of the total.

DOMESTICATION

The domestication of the Norway rat is thought to be associated with the now banned, early nineteenth century spectacle known as rat-baiting. Bets were placed on the time required for a trained terrier, a "ratter", to kill a standard number of rats released into a large pit. These events created a need to capture and to breed wild rats and, subsequently, an opportunity for inquisitive individuals to tame the more distinctive rats, such as the albino, black, and pie-bald, or spotted mutants. By the late 1800s, lines were developed for research purposes in Europe and the United States, and fancy rats were being bred and shown in England. A distinction must be made between domestication and taming. Domestic rats are not tamed wild rats. The process of domestication involves selective breeding and propagation of desirable traits. These traits might include high reproductive rates, certain coat colors, rapid growth, and even behavioral attributes, such as docility or learning ability. In contrast, taming is a process that involves the changing of an individual's behavior without changing its genetic background.

Although rats have been domesticated relatively recently, selective breeding is quite powerful after just a few years because of their short generation time of 13 weeks. One hundred years, or 40 generations, for rats would be equivalent to 10,000 years for humans. As consequence to domestication, the domestic rat attains puberty earlier than the wild Norway rat, displays little evidence of a seasonal sexual cycle, has a larger body weight, an increased litter size, and a more docile disposition. Wild rats live as long as four or five years, whereas the domestic rat rarely exceeds a life span of three years.

TAXONOMIC CLASSIFICATION OF THE NORWAY RAT

Kingdom: Animal
Phylum: Chordata (having a notochord)
Subphylum: Vertebrata (having a vertebral column)
Class: Mammalia (having mammary glands that produce milk to nurse young)
Subclass: Theria (having a placenta)
Infraclass: Eutheria (having an allantoic placenta)
Order: Rodentia (having one pair of incisors and including mice, rats, voles, lemmings, woodchucks, hamsters, gerbils, squirrels, beavers, porcupines, guinea pigs, chinchillas, capybaras, etc.)
Suborder: Myomorpha (including mouse-like rodents and distinguished by jaw muscles and the lack of premolar teeth)
Superfamily: Muroidea
Family: Muridae (including Old World rats and mice and distinguished by the jaw muscles and the structure of the molar teeth)
Subfamily: Murinae
Genus: *Rattus*
Species: *norvegicus*

Rats used in the bloody sport of baiting were wild rats that were caught or specially bred for this purpose. Above and below: the most famous ratter, Billy, rendered by G. Hunt (1823, London). Illustrations courtesy of Dr. Dieter Fleig, The History of Fighting Dogs.

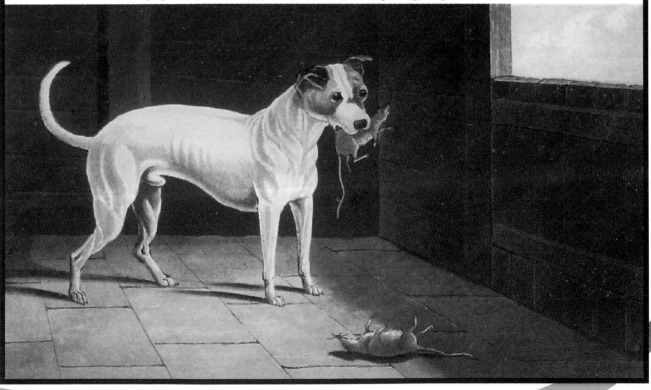

EXTERNAL ANATOMY & GENERAL PHYSIOLOGY

TEETH

The most characteristic feature of rats is the four prominent, orange incisor teeth. These teeth are essential for gnawing. In fact, the name rodent is derived from the Latin verb *rodere*, meaning to gnaw. Rats are said to exert 24,000 pounds per square inch, enough pressure to gnaw through wood, plaster, cinder block, or soft metals such as lead.

The incisor teeth grow throughout the entire life span of the rat at a rate of about 4 to 5 inches a year. The proper length is maintained by the grinding of the upper incisors against the lower incisors. If the jaws are not properly aligned or the teeth are fractured, the teeth

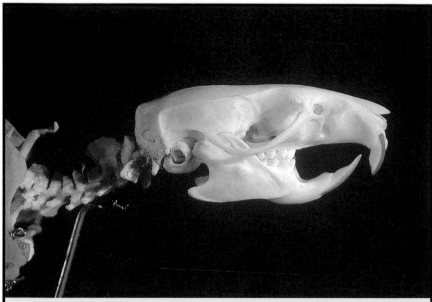

Rat skull. The space between the incisor and the three molar teeth on each side of the jaw is called the diastema. This gap is due to the absence of canine and premolar teeth.

The sharp, angular or chisel-like edges of the incisor teeth are created due to the presence of the hard enamel only on the front surfaces and not on the back surfaces.

may not wear properly and subsequently overgrow. Rats given only powdered or ground meal research diets do not typically have problems with overgrown teeth.

Rats have no second incisor, canine, or premolar teeth. There is a distinct gap, called the diastema, between the incisor and the molar (or cheek) teeth. The diastema allows the lips to withdraw into the mouth, preventing ingestion of particles while the rodent is gnawing on inedible materials. There are three upper and three lower molars on each side of the jaw. All teeth are permanent teeth; there are no deciduous teeth.

Rats are susceptible to dental caries or cavities when fed a high (approximately 60%) sugar diet and in the presence of the common oral bacterium S*treptococcus mutans*. Appropriately, rats were used in research studies that showed the effectiveness of fluoride in the prevention of cavities.

FACE

The upper lip is split by a vertical cleft that extends between the nares of the nose. The pointed snout is quite mobile, sensitive to touch, and has a surface ridged in a pattern that is unique to each animal and is similar to your fingerprints.

The ears are covered by fine hairs. For identification purposes in the research laboratory, the ears may be marked with a small hole or notch or a small metal band.

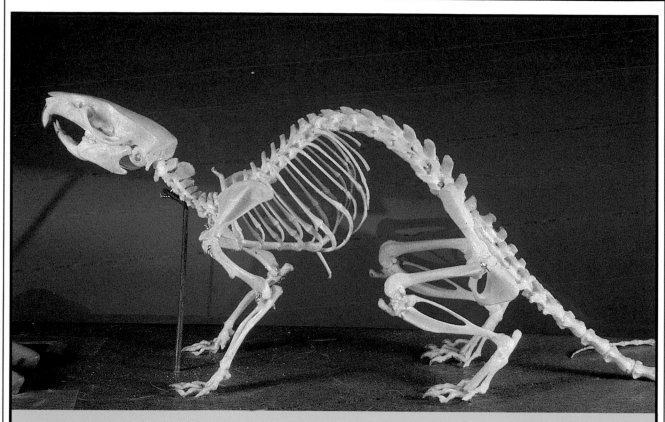

Skeleton of a rat. The rat has 7 cervical, 13 thoracic, 6 lumbar, 4 sacral, and 27 to 30 caudal (or coccygeal) vertebrae.

LIMBS

Rats are quadrupeds with slightly larger hindlimbs than forelimbs. The forelimbs are agile and able to hold and manipulate objects such as seeds.

The front and hind feet all have five digits. All digits are clawed except for the first digit on the forelimbs which is called the thumb or pollex. The pollex has a small, flat nail and is also reduced to two finger bones called phalanges. The other digits each have three phalanges.

Walking pads are present on the feet.

TAIL

The long, rasp-like tail is slightly shorter than the combined length of the head and body.

The powerful tail is used for orientation on the ground and balance during jumping. Young, healthy rats usually land on their feet after a jump.

The naked tail is also important as the principal organ for losing excessive body heat through the dilation of blood vessels. Researchers have seen shorter and fatter tails in rats raised in colder temperatures (10°C or 50°F). This reduction in tail surface area is a physiological adaptation to conserve heat. A tail tattoo is sometimes used to identify a rat, especially in research animals.

SKELETON

The rat is slower than most other mammals in bone maturation. The skeleton of adult rats, particularly males,

This young Siamese male rat is able to climb on a rope using its tail for balance and its prehensile front and hind feet to pull itself up.

continues to grow and does not become completely ossified until after one year of age.

GAIT AND POSTURE

The normal gait is parallel to the floor with the head horizontal, the abdomen just above the floor, and the anus near the floor. There is a slight up-and-down movement with each step. As the rat walks on the full soles of its feet, like bears and humans, the gait is called plantigrade, in contrast to the digitigrade gait of horses and cattle.

The normal postures are sitting upright on its haunches when awake or lying on its side or curled up when asleep or resting. When curious, the rat may rear, rising up on its hind legs and supporting itself using its tail as a third leg.

SEX DIFFERENTIATION

The sexes can readily be distinguished by examining the distance between the outlet of the urinary tract, termed the urethral opening, and the anus. This distance is longer in males. Also, in adult males, even if the rat is cold or frightened and the testes are retracted into the abdomen, the wrinkled sparsely-haired scrotum is quite evident at the base of the tail. In female rats, there are three pairs of pectoral and three pairs of inguinal mammary glands. Male rats lack nipples and have a baculum or *os penis*.

COAT AND EYE COLOR GENES

Coat and eye color genes are well studied in rats. By convention, a recessive gene is designated by an abbreviation starting with a lowercase letter

(*e.g.*, d = dilute) and the alternative dominant gene is designated by a corresponding abbreviation starting with an uppercase letter (*e.g.*, D = non-dilute) or the plus symbol (+) for wild-type.

The wild rat is a light-bellied brown agouti on the back with a light cream or whitish belly. Agouti hairs have alternating dark and light bands such as brown and yellow bands. Some rats may be piebald or spotted. Hooded rats are piebald animals with white fur except for the head and anterior body (thus, the "hood") and for a stripe down the back. Variants of hooded rats include the Berkshire, with white only on the belly, chest, and feet, and the Irish, with white only on the chest and feet.

Some coat color genes and

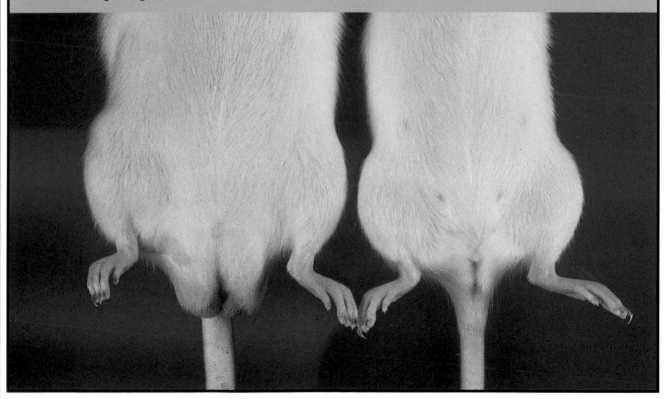

Ventral view of male and female six-month-old rats. In the female, the distance is greater between the urethral opening and the anus.

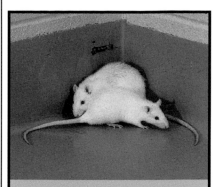

Six-month-old female (in front) and male (in back) albino rats (aaBBccDDhh). In male albinos, the white coat often becomes yellow and oily with age. Also, note that the male is larger.

their symbols are agouti (A), non-agouti (a), non-brown (B), brown (b), albino (c), non-albino (C), Himalayan (c^h), dilute (d), yellow (e), fawn (f), non-hooded (H), hooded (h), silvering (s) and sand (sd).

If a rat is an albino, it has the pair of the genes "cc", which masks the other color genes even if they are dominant genes. Genotypes ccbb, ccBb and ccBB make an albino animal; Ccbb and CCbb make a brown animal; and, CcBB, CcBb, CCBb or CCBB make a black animal.

The normal pigmented (CC or Cc) rat has pigmented eyes. The albino (cc) has red eyes. Other eye mutant genes include ruby-eyed dilute (c^d), pink-eyed dilution (p), ruby-eyed dilution (p^m), and red-eyed dilution (r). Corresponding dominant genes for black eyes are designated P and R. As well as affecting eye color, the mutant genes also dilute coat colors.

COAT TYPE

Coat type mutants and their gene symbols include curly (Cu-1 or Cu-2), fuzzy (fz), shaggy (Sh), kinky (k), rex (Re), masked (mk), cowlick (cw), hairless (hr), hypotrichosis (hy), atrichosis (at), and naked (n).

DIURNAL ACTIVITY

The rat has a daily physiologic rhythm. A rat is most active and eats mostly during the dark hours, and it digests, rests, and sleeps during the light hours. As soon as the lights are switched off, most rats start scurrying about the cage,

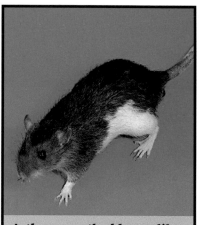

A three-month-old non-dilute brown agouti hooded male rat (AAbbCCDDhh).

foraging for food, and playing. During the light hours, when disturbed, your rat will frequently greet you with a yawn and stretch as it may have been sleeping or is just drowsy. Typically, the higher the light intensity and the longer the light period, the less active rats will be, and vice versa.

VISION

The rat has bulging eyes, an anatomical feature that aids in peripheral vision. However, like most nocturnal animals, its overall eyesight is poor. In fact, a blind rat or a rat with severe cataracts may act essentially normal in a familiar environment such as its own cage.

The rat lacks color vision and is blind to long-wave red light. Dim red lighting can be used to observe the natural behavior of rats during the dark hours.

Due to their having unpigmented irises, albino rats are very sensitive to light intensity. They will have retinal damage and may become blind if exposed to bright lights (over 100 lux or 10 foot-candles) for longer than 16 hours daily. Dim light levels of 32 to 40 lux (3.0 to 3.7 foot-candles) are considered safe for albino rats.

TOUCH

The rat has an excellent sense of touch. Long sensory hairs called vibrissae, or whiskers, are found above the eyes, on the cheeks, and under the chin. They help guide the rat in the dark when it is most active and when it cannot see very well. In addition, scattered over the coat, there are smaller sensory hairs that are also sensitive to

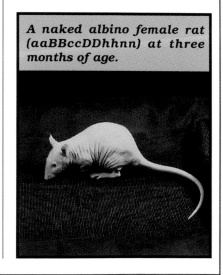

A naked albino female rat (aaBBccDDhhnn) at three months of age.

touch and air currents. These specialized hairs guide the wild rat as it maneuvers through burrows and along walls.

HEARING

Hearing is relatively good over a wide range. The rat can hear high frequencies of up to 80,000 hertz in the ultrasonic range. For contrast, in humans, the average pitch limits are 20 and 20,000 hertz. For rats, the maximum sensitivity of hearing is in the range from 15,000 to 25,000 hertz. Noises above 90 decibels are stressful to rats and may decrease fertility and may even lead to infanticide.

SMELL

Rats have a keen sense of smell. The olfactory areas of the brain are well developed.

Rats use scents, or pheromones, as chemical messages that prompt specific responses especially in reproduction. Group-housed females may become synchronized in their heat, or estrous, cycles when a male is introduced into the cage. This response to male pheromones is called the

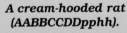

A cream-hooded rat (AABBCCDDpphh).

"Whitten effect," and it is not as strong in rats as it is in mice. Male rats are also attracted to the urine of females that are sexually receptive.

Overall, the natural scents of rats are mild and not offensive to most human noses. Depending on the diet and bedding, there may be a sweet natural odor of wood. Odor problems tend to arise from cages only when they become damp or are not cleaned and sanitized at sufficient intervals.

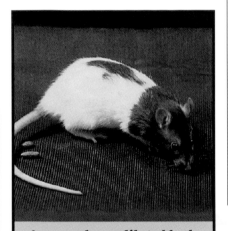

A normal non-dilute black-hooded female rat (aaBBCCDDhhNN or aaBBCcDDhhNN) at three months of age.

TASTE

The rat is believed to not be able to taste water. Unlike in the dog, cat, and pig, water taste receptors have not been identified in the rat. However, rats can taste all possible foodstuffs, and they develop certain preferences. All rats like sweets.

COPROPHAGY

Coprophagy is a behavior in which an animal ingests its own feces. This is a normal and beneficial behavior for rats as well as for most other

A naked non-dilute black-hooded female rat (aaBBCCDDhhnn or aaBBCcDDhhnn) at three months of age.

rodents and for rabbits. Coprophagy has a twofold purpose: (1) to maintain normal gut bacteria by reinoculation of the upper gastrointestinal tract and (2) to capture nutrients, notably the water soluble vitamins and vitamin K, which are synthesized by microbes in the lower gastrointestinal tract. Coprophagy is a behavior seen in animals with hindgut fermentation. Such animals include the rat, with its large cecum and colon. It is not observed in ruminants that have foregut fermentation. The feces ingested by coprophagic animals is a softer, less formed version in contrast to the dry, hard waste pellets.

DEFECATION AND URINATION

Rats do not have great toilet manners. They seldom urinate or defecate in only one spot of the cage. And, particularly when nervous, rats will urinate and defecate while outside the cage.

Fecal pellets in the cage should be firm, dark brown, and elongated with a rounded end. Color can vary with the diet. When nervous and outside their cage, rats sometimes defecate soft, sticky, and smelly feces. This is the stuff that the rat would probably prefer to reingest by coprophagy but the nervousness got in the way.

Diarrhea is not common in pet rats. Prolonged bouts of very soft or runny stool that stain the rat's hind end is often a sign of a medical problem and should be brought to the attention of a veterinarian.

Urine should be clear and yellow. Red urine may mean that there is cystitis or inflammation of the bladder.

GROOMING BEHAVIOR

Healthy rats spend a considerable amount of time each day grooming. They groom and wash their coats using water or saliva to wet their paws and wash their faces. They bend to lick the fur of back flanks, abdomen, and genitalia. To lick the tail and hind legs, rats grasp them in their hands. The hind toes are used to scratch the head and neck areas.

Rats are not dirty animals. In fact, the presence of dirt or foreign odors on the skin stimulates immediate grooming behavior.

THERMOREGULATION

Rats do not tolerate excessive heat well. Sweat glands are absent in the skin and rats do not pant. When hot, a rat salivates and wets its coat for evaporative cooling. It is important not to place your rat's cage too near a window or lamp that may overheat your animal. Wild rats will seek relief from the heat by behavioral means such as burrowing.

Above: *Young Siamese and chocolate rats. The Siamese (AABBc^{h}c^{h}DD) has a medium beige coat color with rich dark sepia points and ruby eyes. The chocolate (aabbCCDD) has a dark chocolate coat with black eyes.* **Below:** *Rex rats have short, curly hair, and even the vibrissae may be curly. This brown agouti female rat (AABBCCDDhhRere) is pregnant.*

Rats adapt to cold by increasing heat production through metabolism of brown fat and behavioral mechanisms. They do not hibernate like some species of hamsters and other animals.

USEFUL CONVERSION VALUES

Mass (Weight):
1 gram (g) =
0.00353 ounce (oz)
1 kilogram (kg) =
2.205 pounds (lb)
1 ounce (oz) =
28.350 grams (g)
1 pound (lb) =
0.454 kilograms (kg)

Length:
1 centimeter (cm) =
0.394 inch (in)
1 meter (m) =
39.370 inches (in)
1 inch (in) =
2.540 centimeters (cm)
1 foot (ft) =
30.480 centimeters (cm)

Volume:
1 milliliter (ml) =
 0.0338 fluid oz
1 liter (l) =
1.057 quarts (qt)
1 liter (l) =
0.264 U.S. gallons (gal)
1 teaspoon (tsp) =
5 milliliters (ml)
1 tablespoon (tbsp) =
15 milliliters (ml)
1 fluid oz (fl oz) =
29.573 milliliters (ml
1 cup (c) =
0.237 liters (l)
1 U.S. gallon (gal) =
3.785 liters (l)

Temperature:
Celsius (°C) =
(°F - 32) x 5/9
Fahrenheit (°F) =
(°C x 9/5) + 32

SELECTED NORMAL DATA

Adult body weight, male:	300-900 grams
Adult body weight, female:	200-500 grams
Body temperature:	96.6-99.5°F (35.9-37.5°C)
Breathing rate:	75-115/minute (94 average)
Heart rate—adult:	261-600/minute (382 average)
Heart rate—newborn:	81-241/minute (161 average)
Life span:	2-3.5 years
Food consumption/day:	5 grams/100 grams body weight
Water consumption/day:	8-11 ml/100 grams body weight
Breeding onset, male:	65-110 days (weight 250-300 grams)
Breeding onset, female:	65-110 days (weight 200-250 grams)
Estrous cycle length:	4 or 5 days
Duration of heat (estrus):	10-20 hours
Time of ovulation:	8-11 hours after onset of estrus
Length of pregnancy (gestation):	21-23 days
Litter size:	6-16 pups
Birth weight:	5-6 grams
Weaning age:	21 days (40-50 grams)
Breeding duration:	350-440 days
Sexual senescence:	450-500 days

Under the heat of floodlights, this five-month-old female black-hooded rat wets her coat with saliva and grooms herself.

ACQUIRING A RAT

SOURCES

Rats are available for purchase at many retail stores. Many stores obtain their rats from fanciers, but some stores purchase rats from suppliers who also sell to researchers.

GENERAL RECOMMENDATIONS

When acquiring a new rat, look for an alert, active animal with even, orange incisor teeth, bright eyes, smooth coat, and no nasal or ocular discharge or diarrhea. The rat should be at the proper weight for its age. All of the animals in the cage should appear healthy and well cared for.

INBRED VERSUS OUTBRED

Rats are available as inbred strains or outbred stocks.

Outbred animals are produced by random matings or matings designed to maintain maximum genetic variation. Outbred animals tend to grow bigger and to be more robust than inbred animals due to an increase in physiologic adaptability referred to as *hybrid vigor*. Most of the rats used in the pet market are outbred.

Inbred animals are those which have minimal genetic variation as a result of brother x sister matings for at least 20 successive generations or an equivalent breeding system (for example, parent x offspring). The physical, physiological, and behavioral characteristics of inbred strains can be predicted. This degree of uniformity can be useful in some research studies.

SHIPPING CRATES

When shipping rats via commercial routes, specially designed crates must meet certain standards or regulations established by transportation associations.

This crate contains lab block diet and baked potatoes. The baked potatoes provide food and moisture. A nutritional gelatin is another good source of food and water. Some crates have a water bag with a sipper tube.

A clean cardboard box, cat carrier, or cage will serve for transporting a few rats a short distance home from the store.

Shipping crates for rats have wire-screened ventilation windows, absorbent contact bedding, food, and a source of water. For specific disease-free animals, crates have a filter covering the outside of the screened windows.

HEALTH BACKGROUND

Some rats are available with a defined health background; that is, they are guaranteed to be free of certain diseases or "specific pathogen-free" (SPF). This is especially important in rats for research. Some viruses (for example, coronaviruses, parvoviruses, and paramyxoviruses) produce minimal or acute diseases and might as well be contracted and recovered from while young. Other disease agents (for example, *Mycoplasma pulmonis*, some bacteria, and most parasites) are best kept excluded from any colony, research or pet, as they cause chronic health problems.

To maintain their disease-free status, SPF rats must be kept separate from the more conventional rats.

QUARANTINE

If you already own one or more rats and you acquire a new one, you should isolate or "quarantine" the new animal in a separate room. A one- to two-week quarantine serves to let you evaluate the health status of a new rat before introducing it to the rest of your rats. A new animal is often stressed by shipping and the changing of the diet, the husbandry procedures, and the environmental conditions. Stress may bring out disease that had been incubating without symptoms at the time of purchase.

Caring for quarantined animals should be done after the care of established animals to protect the latter. Limit your contact with a quarantined animal and, at minimum, wash your hands after handling it. Shared materials (such as cages, feeders, etc.) should be disinfected between rooms.

HUSBANDRY

CAGING

Any cage should be well built, free of sharp edges, easy to clean, and of sufficient size to provide for freedom of movement and normal postural adjustments.

Rats may be kept in cages with solid walls called "shoebox" cages, cages made entirely of wire mesh, or a combination of the two. The solid walls should be of plastic, glass (such as an aquarium), or metal. Walls should not be made of wood, as wood absorbs water and urine and is difficult to sanitize. Metal walls and wire mesh are preferably made of stainless steel, but more commonly, galvanized iron or steel hardware cloth is used for pet rats, as either costs less than stainless steel.

Shoebox cages require some form of contact bedding, while wire caging needs a pan under the cage to collect the droppings. In the pan, cardboard, paper pads, newspapers, or loose bedding may be used to absorb urine, spilled water, and feces.

As wire mesh floors may be uncomfortable and expose the animal to drafts, shoebox cages with wire lids are preferred. Also, in solid bottom cages, the animal can be easily removed without its clinging to the wire floor.

Shoebox cages are a must for pregnant rats and rats with litters. The bedding is needed to help the pups conserve heat. White translucent plastic shoebox cages are typically used to minimize visual disturbances during whelping and nursing.

As rats can jump and climb, cages require a cover. Wire bar, perforated metal, or wire screens that drop on or slide onto the top of the cage may be used.

A hide box or resting box may be appreciated by your pet.

BEDDING

Bedding material is placed inside shoebox cages or on trays beneath cages with wire mesh floors. The bedding serves to absorb urine, feces, and spilled water. Contact bedding also provides both insulation and nesting materials. Bedding increases the animal's comfort when lying down and probably decreases boredom in that the animal can manipulate it. As rats are natural burrowers, when nervous, they sometimes stick their heads in the bedding.

Many different materials are suitable for bedding as long as they are safe and provide a large surface area for evaporation of absorbed fluid. The most common materials include hardwoods such as maple, aspen, or birch shavings or chips. Wood products should be dust free and without splinters and not sawdust. Shredded, clean newspaper, soft cardboard, ground corncobs, and loose hay are also used. Cedar and pine are not recommended as they contain aromatic oils that are mildly toxic. Some wood products are treated with chlorophyll or lemon to mask odors, and some paper products contain antibiotics (neomycin) to reduce the growth of bacteria that

Four Paws Safety Screen Covers are designed to fit any size tank. The locking system ensures the pet's safety. Photo courtesy of Four Paws.

Stainless steel wire mesh cage and clear plastic shoebox cage. The plastic shoebox cage has a wire-bar cover that holds lab block diet and a water bottle. A water bottle is also attached on the side of the plastic cage.

contribute to odors. Do not use cat litter or clay as they are too dusty. Do not use cotton wool or rags, as threads may wrap around the animal's legs and subsequently injure them.

Bedding should be changed as often as necessary to keep odor minimal and the rats dry and clean. One to three bedding changes per week are usually sufficient, depending on the size of the cage and the size and number of rats in the cage.

Dust can be a problem in bedding. Dusty bedding can

To house pet rats, glass aquaria or terraria with screened tops are commonly used. Be sure that the top is secure.

result in inhalation of materials that lead to bacterial and fungal infections in the nasal passages and lungs.

A filter top may be used to control dust emissions in a

shoebox cage. However, a filter top will also affect the air quality within the cage; a decrease in ventilation usually results in increases in both the humidity and the ammonia levels inside the cage.

FEEDERS

Feeders should be durable and should be designed to prevent waste and contamination with bedding, urine, and feces.

Glass, ceramic, metal, or heavy plastic jars or bowls

Bedding products: aspen shavings and maple chips.

may be used for loose feed. A food dish should be heavy or secured to prevent tipping.

Pelleted feed can be best provided in a metal, hanging food hopper. The width of the mesh or slots in the hopper

Brown agouti rats in a metal cage with #2 (two wires per inch or four holes/square inch) wire mesh floor and a pan with pine shavings. Cardboard or paper pads can also be placed under the wire mesh floors.

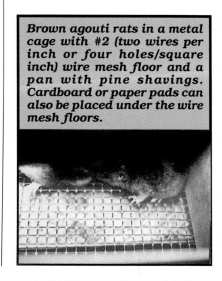

Stainless steel food hopper with pelleted rat feed commonly used in research facilities.

Select food bowls that are sturdy and not liable to tip.

A research animal rack with integrated plastic shoebox cages and automatic watering system. The cages slide on below each perforated shelf.

needs to be wide enough to allow passage of the incisor teeth and snout of the largest rat.

WATER

Ordinarily, rats should be provided with fresh, uncontaminated, potable drinking water at all times, that is, *ad libitum.* If you would not drink the water, do not offer it to your rat.

Rats must have access to fresh clean water at all times. Water bottles that feature stainless steel sipper tubes are an ideal choice.

The water containers should preferably be made of light, translucent, unbreakable plastic; glass bottles are a second choice. Water bottles with plastic or stainless steel screw caps are preferred over rubber stoppers, which will be gnawed and need to be replaced. The stainless steel drinking (or sipper) tubes are preferable to the glass sipper tubes, which can be dangerous to you and your pet if they break. The sipper tube should be positioned away from the bedding, but it must be within reach of the smallest rat.

Water bottles should be checked daily for leaks and should be refilled as needed. They should be washed weekly or when needed. An air leakage or contact of the sipper tube with bedding can result in flooding of a shoebox cage. When filling the water bottle, use fresh tap water and leave a little air in the bottle to prevent lockage of the water flow.

Dehydrated rats will not eat, will lose weight, will have loose, inelastic skin, and often will have dry red crusts around the eyes and nose, a general sign of stress. Dehydration is usually the result of a malfunction in the watering system, such as a lockage or faulty ball valve. In addition, severe illness and medications added to the water can also cause dehydration.

SANITATION

Cages should be cleaned and disinfected at least weekly for

Narrow- and wide-mouth plastic water bottles with rubber stoppers and stainless steel sipper tubes. Sipper tubes function by having a constricted opening or a ball valve to prevent water seepage into the cage.

solid wall cages and every other week for wire mesh cages. First scrub the cage with warm water and a mild detergent (such as hand dishwashing liquid) to clean the cage. Most disinfectants are not effective when used in the presence of excessive organic matter. A hospital disinfectant or general-purpose chemical disinfectant or just very hot water (as found in most automatic dishwashers) can destroy fungi, bacteria, and viruses. Common household bleach (5.25 per cent sodium hypochlorite solution) diluted 200 ml to 4 liters with water is a good disinfectant. However, chlorine is a powerful oxidizing agent and may cause corrosion of metal surfaces. Be sure to thoroughly rinse the cage free of any residual soap or chemical disinfectant to prevent harm to the animals.

Maintaining clean cages and adequate room ventilation helps to control human allergies to animal dander and urinary proteins. Some people develop cutaneous and respiratory allergies to rats as well as to other animals.

VENTILATION

Fresh air is of great importance to supply adequate oxygen and to remove heat, dust, and waste gases.

Ammonia is a waste gas that is naturally made by the bacterial breakdown of urea in urine. The odor of ammonia in a room indicates that the rats are either being kept in poorly

A young chocolate female rat about to use its wooden seesaw.

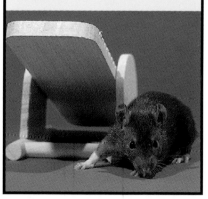

A young Siamese male rat using a stainless steel ball point sipper tube. Ball-point tubes provide cleaner water by reducing the backflow of bacteria and debris into the water bottle.

ventilated, overcrowded conditions or that the cages are not being adequately cleaned. High levels of ammonia may contribute to respiratory disease in rats.

TEMPERATURE AND HUMIDITY

The rat can be bred and maintained at temperatures between 65 to 79°F (18 to 26°C). For rats in wire mesh cages and without bedding, room temperatures should not fall below 70°F (21°C), and drafts should be avoided. Food consumption will decrease and water consumption will increase as the ambient temperature rises.

The relative humidity inside the cage should be between 40% and 70%. Low humidity levels are more frequently a problem in the winter and can be a cause of ringtail in young rats.

LIGHT AND NOISE

Lighting should be dim to moderate, 75-125 foot-candles (807-1345 lux). Bright lighting should be avoided especially for albino animals, which are susceptible to retinal damage since they do not have a pigmented iris to block light.

Lighting cycles must include a dark phase each day. Continuous light can cause retinal damage and reproductive problems. Long days with 14 hours of light may improve reproductive performance.

Sudden noises and vibrations can induce stress in any rat and even cannibalization of newborns by nervous mothers. Some people keep on some light background music to get their animals accustomed to routine amounts of noise.

A young Siamese male rat on a rotating platform for exercise.

Young cream, brown agouti, and black-hooded rats playing on a wooden jungle gym. Toys such as this provide exercise and environmental enrichment.

ENVIRONMENTAL ENRICHMENT

Housing for rats should utilize vertical as well as horizontal space. Useful features include ramps leading to feeding platforms plus visual barriers and tunnels such as small boxes, cardboard tubes, and tin cans without sharp edges. Commercial plastic tunnel systems or polyvinyl chloride (PVC) pipes or nylon toys and jars may also be used to enrich your rat's environment. Research has shown that rats in an enriched environment actually develop larger brains than those rats in deprived environments (*Scientific American*, February 1972). Toys and physical activities have also been demonstrated to reduce obesity and its related problems.

GROOMING

Normally, a rat will keep itself well groomed and clean. There is no need to brush or bathe a healthy rat or to trim its claws or to clean its ears. However, some fanciers will bathe and then brush their rats with talcum powder before shows. And, large, old rats may develop oily coats especially on their backs, where they have difficulty grooming themselves. An oily or soiled rat may be safely bathed using a pet or baby shampoo. The tips of claws can be trimmed using a toenail clipper. Be sure to avoid the quick, which is the pink center containing blood vessels and nerves. If bleeding starts, use digital pressure for a few minutes until the bleeding stops and/or use styptic powder.

Rats are not adverse to water and are able swimmers.

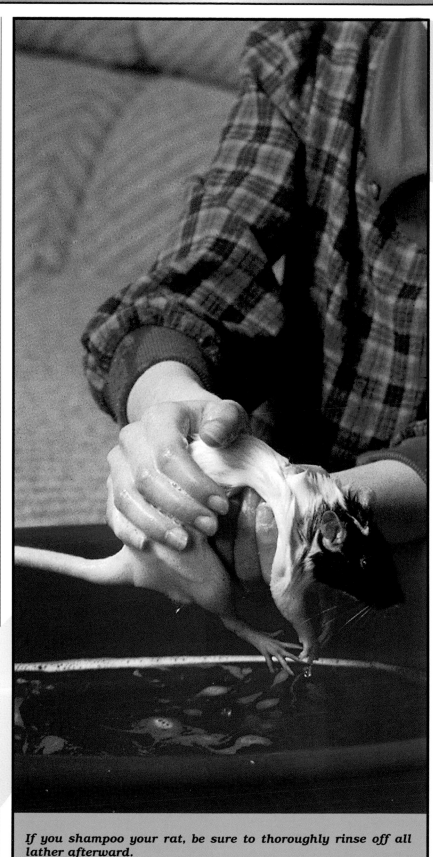

If you shampoo your rat, be sure to thoroughly rinse off all lather afterward.

HANDLING

When picking up a rat, move your hand slowly from behind the animal and grasp the rat with the palm of your hand over the animal's back. Your thumb and index finger should form a circle around the neck and press the rat's forelimbs under its chin. Restraint should be gentle but firm with no sudden hand movements. The grip should not be too tight around the thorax as to impede its breathing. A simultaneous tail grip using your other hand may help stabilize the rat. For large rats, the body should be supported with your other hand. When uncomfortable, a rat may squeal, but it should not be able to bite when held properly.

You can pick up a rat by the *base* of the tail and carry it over a short distance, such as to a nearby cage or to rest on your forearm.

Do not pick up a rat by the *tip* of the tail as the skin may tear off, especially if the rat is heavy and spins. If so, the muscles and ligaments will be exposed and there will be bleeding from the edge of the skin and the muscles. Rats with such tail injuries require veterinary assistance—anesthesia and surgical docking.

Also, when held by the tip of the tail, young rats are agile enough to turn and climb up their tails and possibly bite you.

Do not carry a rat by the skin on the back of its neck. Rats do not have enough loose skin or elasticity to tolerate this grip, and it may also restrict breathing.

Most rats do not like to be held upside down unless conditioned to be held this way.

Pet rats are most commonly handled with the bare hand, while in the laboratory it is good practice to wear gloves to prevent the spread of disease between animals.

The use of forceps or other instruments or heavy cloth, leather, or steel mesh gloves usually will not provide a comfortable or secure hold. Rats may struggle and become hurt, and, consequently, they will

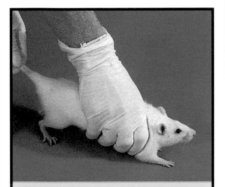

Proper restraint hold for a rat is to grasp the rat from behind with your thumb and index finger, forming a circle around the neck and pressing the rat's forelimbs under its chin.

become less amenable to future handling.

Thin latex, rubber, or vinyl gloves offer good tactile sensitivity and dexterity but have little protective value against a rat's teeth. These thin gloves do provide a warm, secure grip. They are often worn when handling research animals as a good laboratory practice to prevent the spread of microbes or chemicals among animals and from or to animals and people.

Rats that struggle may tear a claw or suffer a nose bleed. You can use some digital pressure to help stop the bleeding from a torn claw. For a nose bleed, the rat is best off when it is returned to its cage to recover on its own.

Sometimes you might drop your rat. Young rats usually manage to land on their feet and usually suffer no injuries. Older, heavy rats can incur bone and teeth fractures from falls.

Overall, the more frequently rats are handled, the more docile they become and the more lenient you can become with your restraint technique.

RAT BITES

When rats bite, it's usually without warning. Rats bite once or momentarily and not repeatedly. Rats are not vicious. Males tend to be more aggressive and to bite more frequently than females. Certain individuals are known biters and warrant warning labels on their cages.

Like most cuts, rat bite wounds should be cleaned with water, a mild antiseptic solution, and, if needed, bandaged. Additional medical attention may be needed if swelling or a discharge develops. Domestic rat bites tend to be less prone to severe infections than cat bites.

To prevent getting bitten, handle your rat gently and every day. Do not startle or tease the animal, and wash any food smell off your hands.

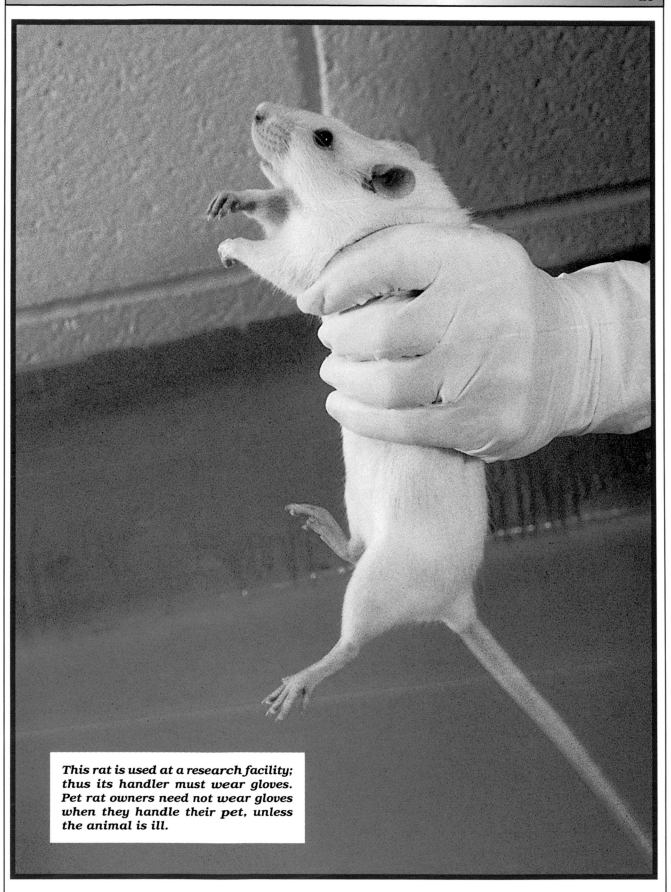

This rat is used at a research facility; thus its handler must wear gloves. Pet rat owners need not wear gloves when they handle their pet, unless the animal is ill.

NUTRITION

FOOD AND WATER

The rat is omnivorous. And, like people, it often prefers junk food high in calories but low in nutritional value. However, feeding is best based on a commercial product formulated for rats or other rodents. Most rodent diets are suitable for rats, mice, gerbils, and hamsters, but not for guinea pigs, as the guinea pig requires vitamin C in its daily diet. On average, a good commercial rat diet contains 14 to 24% protein, 4 to 9% fat, 3 to 11% fiber, 6 to 8% ash, and 60 to 75% carbohydrate.

Rodent diet is available as dry, lab block or pellets or a grain, seed, and biscuit mix. The pelleted variety has the advantage that it can be placed in a suspended hopper, preventing contamination with bedding, etc. Pellets provide a good substrate for gnawing, and pellets can not be picked apart, so the diet remains balanced. Loose mixes are available in regular and gourmet varieties.

Quantities may be purchased from a reputable pet or feed store. Most natural-ingredient dry diets are formulated to provide adequate nutrition for at least six months after the manufacturing date when stored dry and at room temperature, approximately 70°F (21°C). Small amounts may be stored in an air-tight dry container. The bulk may be stored frozen.

Bread, vegetables, cheese, and fresh or dry fruits may be offered as treats. Wash or peel fresh fruits and vegetables well and remove any uneaten fresh food to prevent spoilage. Avoid salty, fatty, and chocolate treats; the latter contains a substance similar to caffeine.

Food and water is usually provided free choice, that is *ad libitum*. However, restricted feeding will prevent obesity and extend the life span for several months, while overfeeding reduces longevity. Adult rats will eat from 12-30 grams of dry feed daily and drink about 2 ml water for every gram of dry feed consumed.

NUTRITIONAL REQUIREMENTS

Although the rat was important in the discovery of vitamin A, vitamin deficiency problems are rare when providing fresh, completely balanced commercial diets.

A dry food mix consisting of oats, sunflower seeds, and bits of dog biscuit. When it comes to your rat's diet, the best thing to do is to stick to the basic rodent mix and occasional fruit/vegetable supplements and alternative foodstuffs from time to time.

Rawhide Oodles, manufactured by Nylabone® Corporation, are healthful snacks for rats and other small mammals.

Good commercial diets are fortified with vitamin A (10 to 40 IU/gram), vitamin D_3 (1 to 5 IU/gram), vitamin E (32 to 67 IU/gram), and thiamin (10 to 17 ppm). In addition, vitamin deficiencies are difficult to induce in the rat, as it gets some vitamins (notably, folic acid, biotin, vitamin K, and vitamin B_{12}) from bacterial synthesis in the intestines and coprophagy. The rat does not require a dietary source of ascorbic acid (vitamin C), as it can synthesize this vitamin in its liver. Vitamin supplements, preferably powdered mixes to sprinkle on food, are needed only for rats on antibiotics or for those eating old and unbalanced diets. A vitamin supplement added to the water may have a taste that discourages the rat from drinking and may also promote the growth of bacteria in the water. Salt or mineral blocks are not needed for normal rats.

The energy requirement of the rat is a function of body weight, ambient temperature, and activity. Rats usually eat for calories. However, if unbalanced diets are provided, rats may become obese through overeating to acquire adequate amounts of essential nutrients. Adult rats usually need 30 to 130 kilocalories (gross energy) per day.

Mention should be made regarding the daily nutritional requirements for breeding female rats. During gestation, the average daily total feed intake of 13 grams increased to a level of 19 grams/day by the twentieth day of gestation in one stock of outbred rats. Following a temporary decrease at whelping, the average food consumption rose to around 40 grams/day at the twentieth day of lactation. During lactation, the average daily consumption was approximately 33 grams per day. Pregnant or nursing females are sometimes given diets supplemented with protein-rich ingredients such as cooked eggs, meats, cheese, and nuts.

For variety, you can offer your pet flavored Oodles.

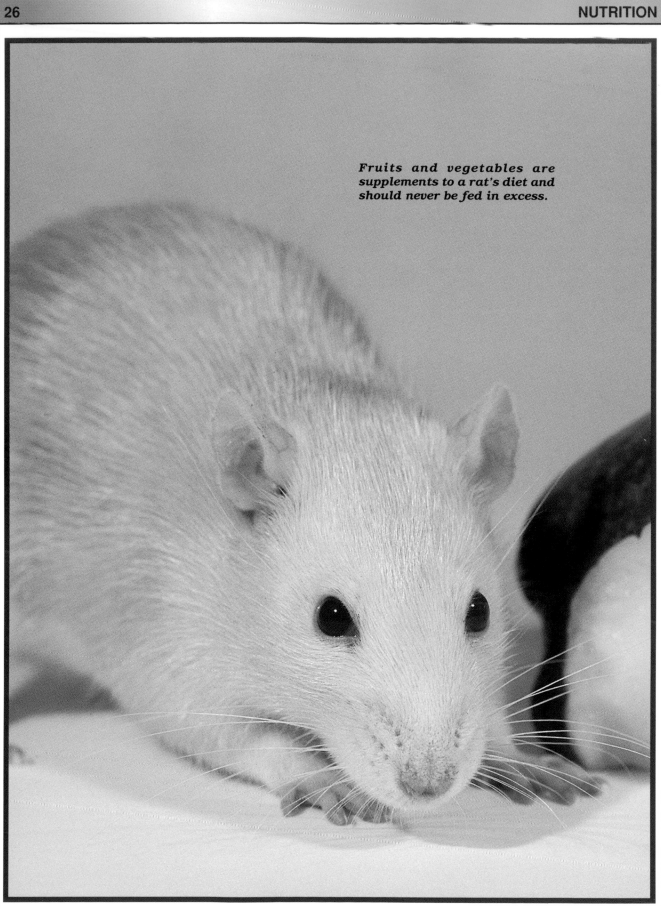

Fruits and vegetables are supplements to a rat's diet and should never be fed in excess.

BEHAVIOR & TRAINING

GENERAL

Domestic rats are known for their gentle and intelligent behavior. Their learning abilities make them useful in studies in the laboratory.

Rats tend to be *neophobic;* that is, they tend to have a fear of new things. Although they are inquisitive, they are cautious when investigating new things in their environment.

WITH HUMANS

Domestic rats have been selectively bred for docility. They have a natural interest and like for humans. Rats of all ages and both sexes are usually easy to handle when handled gently and often and when well fed.

If badly handled or malnourished, a rat will become a biter. Do not mistreat a rat, as it has a good memory. Also, crankiness can be contagious. Nearby rats may become disturbed when they hear others squeal. In addition, rats sense whether someone is apprehensive about handling them.

It is also not wise to wear peanut butter on your fingers when handling rats.

AMONG RATS

Unlike wild rats and many other rodents, domestic rats tend to be non-aggressive with

A young Siamese male rat and a young chocolate female investigating a new toy. Play behavior is greatest in young rats.

Supervise your rat when it is outside of its cage so that it does not chew any electrical cords or cause damage due to its natural inquisitive and gnawing behaviors.

each other. Consequently, rats may be housed individually or in groups.

Rats tolerate single housing well. In fact, rats singly housed have been tested and found to have lower levels of the hormones associated with stress.

Rats may be housed in groups of the same sex or mixed sexes. Group-housed rats exhibit behaviors such as huddling and grooming. Young and group-housed rats often sleep not merely lying alongside each other but often piled together in a heap. However, although female rats with litters will tolerate the presence of their mate, they sometimes will fight with other adult females in the same cage.

Aggression may be seen as chasing, rearing or arched back, raised hair, teeth-chattering, ears pulled backward, boxing, leaping and biting. Bite wounds are often on the back or tail. A submissive rat will collapse on its back and remain motionless. Among fighting rats, either the biting or the bitten animal should be removed.

AMONG OTHER SPECIES

Rats seem to tolerate or can be trained to associate with dogs, cats, rabbits, and other animals, except for other rodents, especially mice, to which they often react with extreme hostility.

ABNORMAL BEHAVIOR

Singly housed females may develop a peculiar

If you are going to provide your rat with an exercise wheel, you must be sure that it is sufficiently large to prevent your rat from getting its tail trapped.

repetitive habit that involves taking the tail in the mouth and carrying it. This "tail-hoarding" behavior may be a sign of boredom, which may be alleviated by the addition of another rat to the cage, or by putting something in the cage to engage the animal's attention. Suitable items for the latter include paper, wood, or nylon toys.

GENERAL ACTIVITY

Activity and play are greatest in young rats. However, adult females become more active when in heat.

Running wheels and rotating platforms are good devices for providing exercise for active rats. These devices may have to be custom made for rats with their long tails. The more readily available hamster wheels are too small and may trap tails.

TRAINING

Rats can be taught to carry out quite complicated manipulations, and this ability has encouraged their use in behavioral research.

Training is best accomplished by procedures known to behavioral psychologists as "operant conditioning." Operant conditioning involves giving rewards (or "positive reinforcement") for desired responses. The best rewards are small food treats, such as cereals (for example, sugar-coated rice crispies) or small candies. The process of rewarding closer and closer steps to the desired response is called "shaping." At each step, rewards must be given immediately and with consistency. It is better *not* to reinforce a correct response

Pet shops stock a variety of Nylabone® products that your pet will enjoy.

Nylabone® products are excellent for satisfying your rat's need to gnaw.

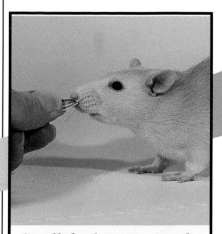

Small food treats can be given as rewards when your pet demonstrates a desired response in its training program.

than to provide the reward too late, when it may confuse the rat. Since providing the treat immediately is difficult, you can train the animal that a treat is to be expected when it hears a noise. Experimental psychologists use a device called a "cricket" clicker.

To help you understand the basic elements of operant conditioning, let's take the following example. Twelve-hour food, but not water, deprivation may be useful to motivate your rat. Start by placing three rice crispies in a dish. When the rat finds the food, begin simultaneously clicking and presenting a single rice crispie only when the rat is moving away from the dish. The goal is to get the rat to associate the clicking noise with a food reward. Eventually, the rat, upon hearing the clicking, will automatically go to the food dish in anticipation of receiving a rice crispie. Do not present the food and noise when the rat has its head in the dish, as this is not reinforcing the desired response.

Once the rat learns how the reward system works, it can be trained to approach and then press a bar or switch in a chamber (the so-called "Skinner box," named after the behavioral psychologist B.F. Skinner who wrote *Behavior of Organisms*, 1938), push a ball up a ramp, pull a line on a balloon, run a race, navigate a maze, walk a tightrope, or other activities.

SHOWS

Rats have been displayed at mouse and rat club shows and at convention center pet shows. These events have been going on in Great Britain for almost a century and in California and New Jersey for the past couple of decades. Animals tend to be judged on general health, physical appearance, and temperament. These shows are useful to improve the

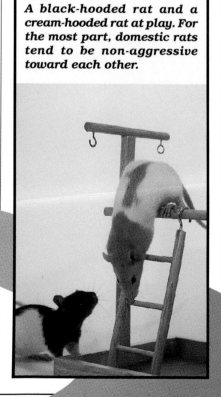

A black-hooded rat and a cream-hooded rat at play. For the most part, domestic rats tend to be non-aggressive toward each other.

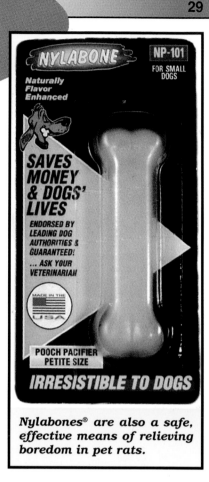

Nylabones® are also a safe, effective means of relieving boredom in pet rats.

public image of rats and to get people together who share similar interests.

Rats are also displayed at public programs dealing with student education. Some schools have public events for students to show off their rats as part of a course with behavioral conditioning projects. In the United States, the National Research Council has principles and guidelines for the use of animals in precollege and college education. To participate in state, national, and international science and engineering fairs, students must follow specific rules for research involving vertebrate animals. According to these rules, rats or any other live vertebrate animal can not be exhibited at science fairs.

REPRODUCTION

ENVIRONMENTAL FACTORS

Domestic rats breed throughout the year with minor seasonal variations. Litter frequency may decrease in the winter in the absence of artificial lighting. Daily lighting of 12 to 14 hours is best for breeding. Constant light for as little as three days may cause problems in female fertility. High room temperatures may reduce male fertility.

BREEDING SYSTEMS

Rats do not pair bond. They may be bred in monogamous pairs or in a polygamous harem mating system with one or more males in a single uncrowded cage. Monogamous mating requires more males and cages but simplifies record keeping. In a polygamous system, each male can service two to nine females. In a communal mating system, females may share nursing duties.

PUBERTY

Sexual maturity is reached by two months of age in both sexes. The testes descend well prior to puberty, usually around days 21 to 28; but they remain retractable throughout life. In the adult male, the testes are usually retracted into the abdomen when the animal is frightened or cold. Breeding is best delayed until both the female and the male are at least 90 days old.

PRODUCTIVITY

Over a typical life span, a female rat can produce a dozen litters, each with six to 18 young, with interbirth intervals of three to six weeks. The size of the litters is affected by genetics and age. Some outbred stocks are known for large litters. A pair of rats can produce 15,000 descendants in their life span.

Rats have a fertile "heat"

A black-hooded dam with two-day-old litter. Eye and skin pigment is evident in the pups.

An albino dam with two-day-old litter. The nest is usually in a corner of the cage. The bedding is heat-dried, ground corn cobs, which provide good insulation for the pups.

within 48 hours after whelping or parturition. Rats bred in monogamous pairs can take advantage of this postpartum heat. If this heat is not utilized, the female rat resumes cycling two to four days after the litter is weaned.

Females will continue to have litters into old age, although they will become less regular after one year and their productivity (such as size of litter, numbers weaned, etc.) will decrease.

ESTROUS CYCLE

Heat, or estrus, occurs usually at night, in a four- to five-day estrous cycle in the adult female rat. Estrus can be detected when the vulva becomes slightly swollen and

The same albino dam pictured above carefully checks on her pups. At birth, the babies are naked, blind, and deaf.

the vagina becomes dry in contrast to the usual moist pink. Female rats in heat are hyperactive and brace themselves when touched. Their ears quiver when they are stroked on the head or back, and touching the pelvic region induces a posture termed *lordosis,* in which the head and rump are raised and the back is arched downward.

MATING

Mating, or copulation, is usually nocturnal. The male will mount the female from the rear. Copulation lasts several seconds. After mating, a white, waxy copulation plug remains in the vagina for up to 12 hours, after which time it will fall out. The copulation, or vaginal, plug is formed mainly from secretions of the

male accessory sex glands, that is, the seminal vesicles, prostate gland, and coagulating gland. If you have wire mesh bottom cages, the plug can often be found in the pan below the cage.

PREGNANCY

Pregnancy, or gestation, lasts for 21-23 days. If the rat was mated at the heat after whelping, simultaneous lactation may delay implantation 3 to 7 days and therefore lengthen gestation to 30 or more days. Abdominal enlargement becomes evident at about two weeks. Mammary development is evident at 14 days. False pregnancy, or pseudopregnancy, is rare in rats.

When using a harem system of mating, pregnant

females are often removed to a separate cage prior to whelping. They may not tolerate the other adult females in the cage while nursing. The adult male may be kept with the adult female in the cage, but it is safer for the litter if the male is removed shortly before parturition and during the lactation period.

Prior to parturition, females show nest-building activity, especially in cooler environments. Expectant mothers pile bedding material to one side of the cage and will shred paper to construct a nest.

WHELPING

Newborn rats, or pups, are delivered one by one at intervals of five to ten

During the first several days after the birth, it is best to avoid unnecessarily disturbing the dam and her litter.

Above: *These pups are very pink and healthy. Milk can be seen through the abdominal wall as a beige area. The umbilicus is a small, brown scab. Below: A hooded rat nursing her litter. During their first few weeks of life, the young receive all of the nourishment that they need from their mother.*

minutes, usually in the early morning. Difficult whelping, or dystocia, is uncommon (and less than 1%). The pups may be born head first or in a breech position. The mother, or dam, cleans the pups and eats the placenta. Stillborn pups and weak pups may also be eaten or they may be left scattered in the bedding. The dam will place the strong, pink-colored pups in the nest area.

PUPS

At birth the young are hairless, blind, toothless, with closed ears and eyelids, undeveloped limbs, and short tail, and weigh five to six grams. Without fur, the pups rely on the dam and adequate bedding for thermoregulation. By five days, they have doubled in body weight and have opened ears. A thin, silky hair is present after seven days. As the hair coat grows, the young become less dependent on maternal body heat. By the tenth day, the pups are covered with fur and may wander around the cage. On days 11-12, their eyes are open, and they have teeth and can eat solid food. The young increase their solid food consumption, while still suckling, until they finally become independent of the dam's milk by 21 days of age, when they can be weaned.

Most dams will allow you to handle the pups from the first day onward, but it is best to minimize disturbances such as handling, changing bedding, and loud noises. Use latex, rubber, or vinyl gloves or a paper towel when handling young. This minimizes foreign odors on the young. Replace any handled young within the nest.

LACTATION

The young begin to suckle within the first three hours. They are guided to the teats by smell. The stomach of a nursing pup can be seen through the thin abdominal wall as a beige-colored structure.

If you do not see milk in the stomachs and the pup appears dry and gray at day two, you have problems. You

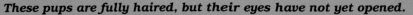

These pups are fully haired, but their eyes have not yet opened.

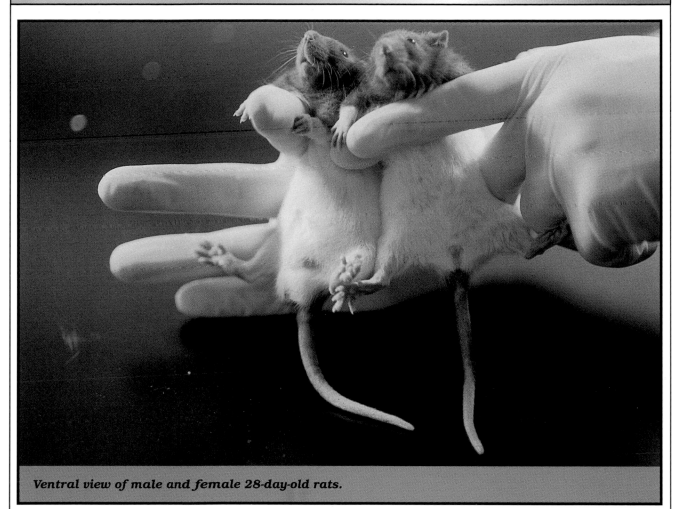

Ventral view of male and female 28-day-old rats.

may need to foster the pup. Fostering pups to another dam is relatively easy and described below. Hand feeding of rats is difficult but sometimes done in research colonies, utilizing milk collected from lactating rats.

Providing the pups with some semisoft feed or mash reduces their dependence on their mother's milk and increases their growth rates. Milk can be mixed with ground diet in a jar lid placed on the floor of the cage.

FOSTERING

Rat pups can be transferred to foster mothers. This is done if the natural dam is ill, lacks milk, has a very large litter, or is just a poor mother. First time or primiparous mothers tend to be more nervous and to have more problems with raising litters, especially large litters over 12 pups.

The best time to foster young is during the first week of life. Only dams with good milk yield should be used as foster mothers, and ideally the pups to be fostered should be of the same age as the litter into which they are to be fostered. The fostered pups are transferred to the new mother and placed within the nest in a way to get them covered with the scent of the natural litter and cage bedding.

SEXING OF PUPS

Determining the sex of the pups can be done by comparing the distance between the genital papillae and the anus. This distance in males is about twice that in the females. In addition, the genital papillae are larger in males. Nipples in the female pups are visible at one week of age. The testes in the male descend into the scrotum by three to four weeks.

BIRTH CONTROL

If you do not want your rats to breed, you must keep them segregated by sex after about seven weeks of age or contact a veterinarian about surgical options.

DISEASES

GENERAL CONSIDERATIONS

Rats are susceptible to noninfectious diseases such as management-related, genetic, metabolic, nutritional, behavioral, aging and cancerous problems and to infectious diseases caused by viral, bacterial, fungal, and parasitic agents.

General signs of ill health include a rough hair coat, loose skin symptomatic of weight loss, stiff-legged gait, arched back or hunched position, lethargy or dullness, labored breathing, sneezing, diarrhea, and decreased food and water consumption.

Certain lines of rats are prone to developing diseases such as diabetes, hypertension, seizures, liver disease, blindness, immunodeficiency syndromes, obesity and cancer. These rats are valuable to researchers in the study of disease processes and in the development of treatments for human and animal diseases.

Below are brief descriptions of the more common health problems. If an animal is ill, you should call a veterinarian, just as you should call a doctor if you are concerned about the health of you and your family.

SPECIFIC DISEASES

Ringtail is the name given to the condition associated with dry, annular constrictions around the tails of young, preweanling rats. Low humidity, below 30%, and cool temperatures, below 60°F (16°C), or more rarely high temperatures above 84°F (29°C), dehydration, nutrition, and genetic susceptibility may predispose young rats to ringtail. Ringtail typically occurs in

A one-week-old pup with ringtail and a normal littermate.

Ringworm in humans is sometimes seen as mild dermatitis, characterized by a gradually extending lesion with a scaling, slightly raised border and healing-to-normal inner area.

the winter, when humidity and room temperatures are likely to be low. Gangrene and subsequent sloughing of the tail occur in severe cases. Treatment consists of improved husbandry, better temperature and humidity control, and topical emollients.

Care must be exercised to prevent **traumatic tail injuries** in domestic rats, whose tail length is up to 65 per cent of the total body length. Do not pick up rats by the tip of the tail, as the skin can tear off. Be careful when placing heavy objects in the cage and when closing cages so that the tail is not crushed. Damaged tails with exposed muscle and ligaments will become dry and may subsequently break off. Your rat will recover faster if veterinary assistance is sought to anesthetize your rat and surgically dock the tail to a length just above the injured area.

Pododermatitis, or inflammation of the feet, may result from unsanitary housing conditions, poorly designed cage flooring, or obesity. Treatment includes topical and/or systemic antibiotics, improvements in habitat sanitation, and utilization of soft bedding materials.

If the upper and lower jaws are not in proper apposition, a condition termed **malocclusion**, the incisor teeth will overgrow. Causes of malocclusion are often multiple and may be of genetic origin or from trauma resulting in broken or lost teeth, or possibly from nutritional imbalance. Although rats on powdered diets do not necessarily have problems with overgrown teeth, the lack of substrate for gnawing is often said to contribute to this problem. Affected animals may show a number of signs, including a gradual

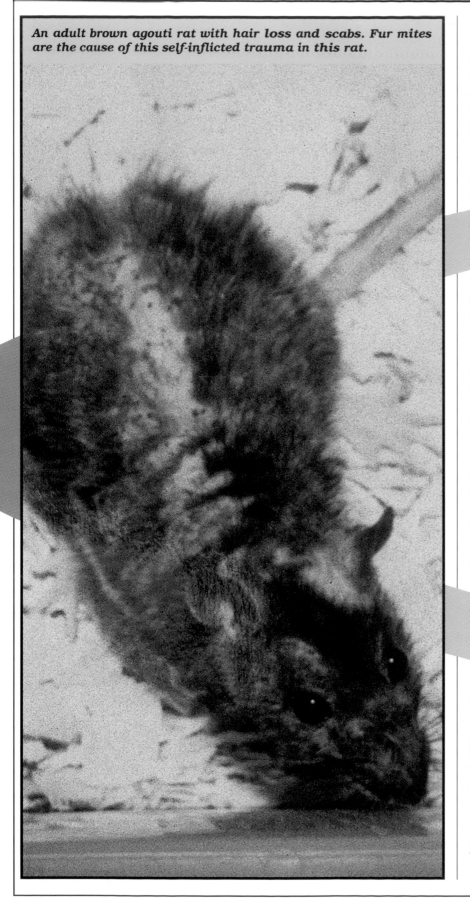

An adult brown agouti rat with hair loss and scabs. Fur mites are the cause of this self-inflicted trauma in this rat.

decrease in food intake that may progress until eating stops completely, a condition called **anorexia**. Another common sign of overgrown teeth is **slobbers**, or excessive drooling of saliva. This condition results in wet, matted fur around the mouth, chin, chest, neck, and forelimbs. Eventually, bacterial skin infections and hair loss may occur. Unless corrected, death usually results because of starvation, infections, or other secondary complications. To correct the situation, the overgrown teeth must be cut to normal lengths using an instrument such as a nail trimmer or wire cutters. However, unless the inciting cause is corrected (which is impossible when genetic), the corrective measure is only temporary, and the teeth will continue to grow abnormally and require trimming possibly on a weekly basis. Animals in which this trait is suspected to be hereditary should not be bred.

Boredom may lead to hair chewing or **barbering**, in which you will see patches of hair loss with shortened hair shafts. Self barbering often occurs on the forelimbs. Barbering may also occur in group-housed rats when a dominant rat barbers subordinate animals. Treatment consists of providing more space and activities and, in the latter case, by removing either the aggressive or subordinate rat.

Ringworm is a fungal infection of the skin. Typically, dermal fungal infections appear as a circular or ring-shaped area of hair loss with broken hair shafts and small crusts or scabs. In rodents, the most common ringworm fungus is *Trichophyton mentagrophytes*, which is transmissible to or from people.

Chromodacryorrhea, or red tears, is commonly seen in sick rats or stressed rats. The red color is due to porphyrin pigments and not to blood. The porphyrin-rich secretion originates from the Harderian gland, which lies behind the rat's eyeball and is named after the Swiss anatomist Johann Jacob Harder (1656-1711). Excessive production or a blockage of drainage leads to an overflow of tears, which dry to form red crusts around the eyes and nares. Often, the forelimbs become stained from face-rubbing. A relatively common coronavirus called sialodacryoadenitis, or SDA virus, will produce inflammation of the tear ducts and chromodacryorrhea. Rats usually recover completely from SDA virus infections within a couple of weeks. Chromodacryorrhea due to

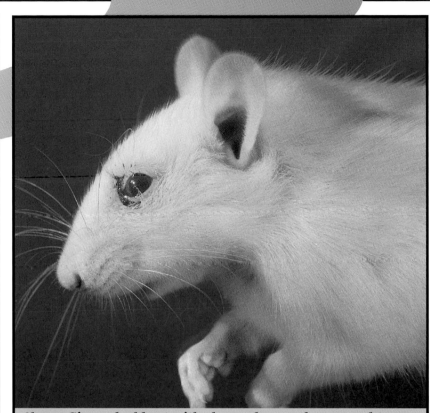

Above: Six-week-old rat with chromodacryorrhea, or red tears. The tear glands are rich in red pigments called porphyrins. When stressed as in illness, from environmental problems, or from dehydration, etc., rats secrete more tears, which can overflow the eyelid margins or flood the nasal cavities. Below: Close-up of the skin of the mite-infested rat seen on the facing page. A veterinarian might culture the skin for the presence of ringworm and staphylococcal bacteria.

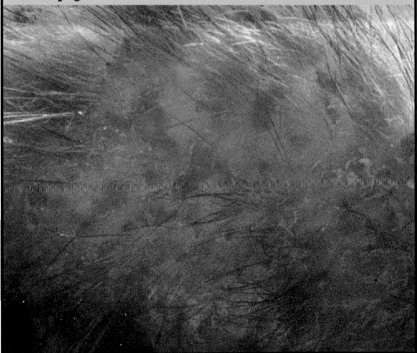

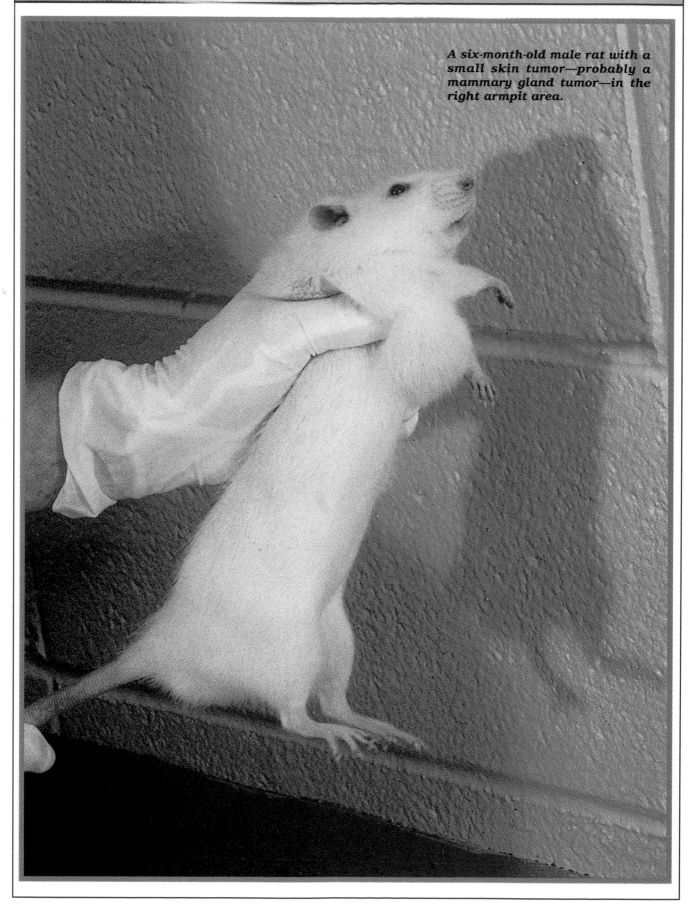

A six-month-old male rat with a small skin tumor—probably a mammary gland tumor—in the right armpit area.

stress such as lack of water usually ceases after the stress has been alleviated.

Several viruses are common in pet rats. Among those that rarely produce illness are the parvoviruses (including Kilham's rat virus, Toolan's H-1, and orphan parvovirus) and the paramyxoviruses (including Sendai virus and pneumonia virus of mice). Sialodacryoadenitis (SDA) virus, a coronavirus, has been mentioned earlier as a cause of chromodacryorrhea. SDA virus also produces inflammation in the salivary glands. This condition is seen as swellings of the ventral head and neck areas. Most rats infected with SDA will self-recover within a week or two.

In general, in old rats, any lumps and bumps are likely to be **tumors**. In rats, even males, the most common tumor is the mammary gland tumor. A mammary gland tumor can occur anywhere from the neck down because rats have extensive areas of mammary gland tissue underneath and on sides of the body. Most mammary gland tumors are benign, that is, they are not very invasive and do not spread. However, mammary gland tumors can grow to a very large size and may become ulcerated and infected.

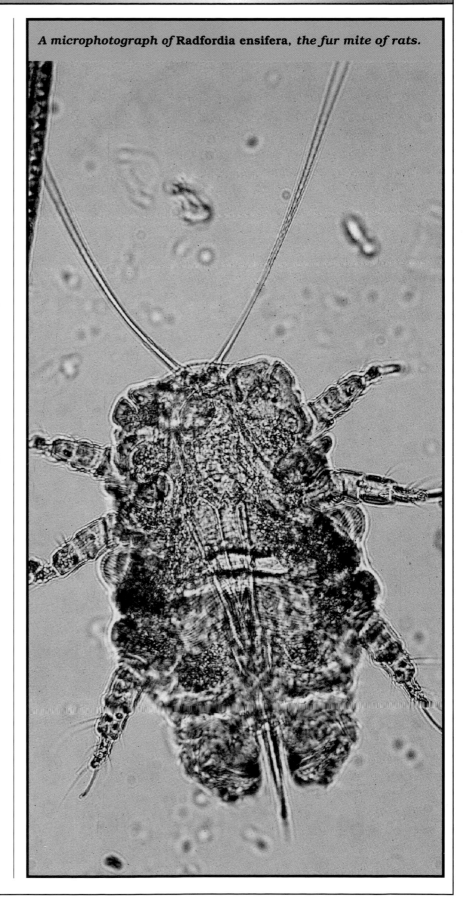

A microphotograph of **Radfordia ensifera,** *the fur mite of rats.*

A thin, old albino rat, rather infirm and listless. As rats reach old age, they are prone to cancer, kidney and heart failure, and degenerative disorders of nerves and muscles.

Mammary gland tumors can be surgically removed, but new ones tend to develop.

Old rats, especially males, are prone to **kidney failure**. Affected rats drink more water and urinate large volumes, as their kidneys are not able to concentrate urine. There is no cure; however, a low-protein diet reduces the incidence of this disease and helps animals with mild kidney failure.

Mycoplasma pulmonis is the cause of **chronic murine pneumonia**, probably the most common and a most serious infectious disease in pet rats. Signs are nonspecific but may include snuffling, head-tilt (due to an inner ear infection), labored breathing, lowered fertility, weight loss, and premature death. Mycoplasmosis often progresses over several months and is nearly impossible to cure. Some improvement may be seen with antibiotics, such as tetracycline in drinking water. Sendai virus and bacteria often complicate *M. pulmonis* infection. Prevention is by acquiring rats that are known to be free of these diseases. This can be determined by serologic testing or by culture. The microbial organism is transmitted at times during birth or by the aerosol route from rat to rat.

This old agouti rex rat has a semi-healed abscess, which has been opened and drained. A scab is now forming. Abscesses are often due to puncture or bite wounds.

Mycoplasma arthritidis is a cause of arthritis in rats.

Ulcerative dermatitis is a condition usually associated with Staphylococcal bacteria. Itchy, moist wounds are seen usually around the shoulders and neck. Self-trauma plays a role in the development of this disease. It is normal for rats, people, and other animals to have some types of staphylococcal bacteria on the skin. Disease tends to be a problem only for certain individuals. Treatment includes topical antibiotic ointment, good sanitation practices, and toenail clipping to reduce injury by excessive scratching.

Streptococcus pneumoniae is a cause of bacterial pneumonia in rats and humans. There are several types, and all are not considered to be acquired from or transmitted to people. Although many rats can be asymptomatic carriers, other rats may have red nasal discharges, hunched postures, difficulty in breathing, abnormal respiratory sounds, anorexia, depressed activity, weight loss, and death. Diagnosis is by culture and identification of the bacteria. Penicillin may be helpful in reducing the severity of the disease, which is difficult to cure.

Streptobacillus moniliformis is a bacteria responsible for **Rat-bite Fever** in people. The disease is now rare among people dealing with rats. Its symptoms in humans may include fever, chills, vomiting, headache, muscle aches, rash, and arthritis. There are no symptoms in rats.

Signs associated with **salmonellosis** in the rat are depressed appetite and activity, rough hair coat, and soft to unformed feces. In recent years, *Salmonella* infections have not been considered too common in domestic rats.

Tapeworms such as *Hymenolepis nana* and *Hymenolepis diminuta* may inhabit the small intestine of several species, including rats, mice, hamsters, and humans. Eggs are passed in the feces. With *H. nana*, the life cycle may be either direct or indirect. In the indirect life cycle, eggs are eaten by an arthropod intermediate host such as grain beetles, fleas, or moths. In this cycle, the tapeworm stays in a larval stage. If a suitable final host ingests an infected insect, the adult tapeworm forms in the intestines. For *H. diminuta*, the intermediate host is essential. Heavy infections can result in poor weight gain and sometimes abdominal distress. Veterinary drugs are needed for treatment.

To prevent tapeworms, rats should not be fed diets contaminated with insects, and habitats should not be infested with insects.

Pinworms are fairly common in rats. Symptoms such as diarrhea, poor weight gain, or anal irritation are only associated with infections by large numbers of worms. The species of pinworms in rats are *Syphacia muris*, *Syphacia obvelata*, and *Aspicularis tetraptera*. Adult pinworms live in the cecum and colon. *Aspicularis* eggs are released in the colon; however, the pregnant female *Syphacia* pinworm migrates outside of the anus to release its eggs. Female *Syphacia* worms are 2 to 4 mm long and 0.1 mm wide, visible to the naked human eye. Diagnosis of infection can be done by microscopic examination of fecal pellets for *Aspicularis* eggs and microscopic examination of clear adhesive tape sampling or skin scrapings of the perianal region for *Syphacia* eggs. Pinworms are difficult to eradicate, as the eggs are light enough to become airborne and thus spread readily, the eggs can survive in the environment for a couple of weeks even in the presence of some disinfectants, and self

reinfection occurs. Modern veterinary drugs are best to kill the adult worms. Rat pinworms are different from the *Enterobius vermicularis* species that infects people.

Mites that burrow in the skin, for example, *Notoedres muris*, may induce scratching with the resultant abrasions and hair loss. Other mites that live in the fur, for example, *Radfordia ensifera*, are usually less bothersome but more prevalent in rats. Veterinary drugs and topical pesticides such as flea and tick shampoos, sprays, and powders can exterminate the mites. These mites are spread by contact among rats and do not affect people.

PREVENTION

Diseases are best prevented by buying healthy animals, quarantining new and sick animals, and good nutrition and general care. Blood tests are available to your veterinarian for the detection of many of the viruses and some of the bacteria-producing diseases in rats.

For the latest and most effective diagnostic techniques and treatments, consult a veterinarian who is familiar with rats.

EUTHANASIA

Owners of companion animals often have to face a difficult decision as to whether or not their pet's life should be terminated. In the

case of a severe illness, owners can choose euthanasia over prolonged suffering. Euthanasia is a word derived from the Greek terms *eu*, for "good," and *thanatos*, for "death." Euthanasia is the act of inducing death without pain or distress. Rats can be humanely killed by someone who has the proper training and equipment. This person is often a veterinarian. Accepted methods of euthanasia for rats include overdose of a gas or injectable anesthetic agent and quick physical methods. Guidelines have been published by the Panel on Euthanasia in the *Journal of the American Veterinary Medical Association*, January 15, 1993.

DEATH

The death of any pet is an unfortunate loss often accompanied by a jumble of feelings —grief, shock, anger, and sadness. A deceased pet was an individual animal that was lucky to have had a caring home.

There are several options for disposal of pets. Most veterinarians can help. Arrangements can be made with a veterinarian, a humane organization, or directly with a pet cemetery or crematory for burial or cremation. Home burial is typically permitted in rural and suburban settings. For burial, the animal's remains are best placed in a plastic bag and then encased in a solid outer container to reduce the scent and chance of animals digging at the grave site.

SOURCES OF ADDITONAL INFORMATION

Baker, H.J., Lindsey, J.R., and Weisbroth, S.H. (eds): *The Laboratory Rat.* Vol I. *Biology and Diseases.* New York: Academic Press, 1980.

Fox., J.G., Cohen, B.J., and Loew, F.M. (eds): *Laboratory Animal Medicine.* Orlando, FL: Academic Press, 1984.

Harkness, J.E., and Wagner, J.E.: *The Biology and Medicine of Rabbits and Rodents,* 4th ed. Philadelphia: Williams & Wilkins, 1995.

Mays, N.: *The Proper Care of Fancy Rats.* Neptune City, NJ: TFH Publications, 1993.

Poole, T. B. (ed): *The UFAW Handbook on the Care and Management of Laboratory Animals,* 6th ed., Longman Scientific & Technical, 1987.

American Association for Laboratory Animal Science (AALAS)
A professional association for technicians veterinarians, managers, sales representatives, and manufacturers involved in the production care and use of the laboratory animal. AALAS publishes *Laboratory Animal Science, Contemporary Topics in Laboratory Animal Science,* and other documents; holds an annual meeting; and certifies technicians.
AALAS, 70 Timber Creek Drive, Cordova, TN 38018. telephone (901) 754-8620.

CLUBS

Readers should note that the addresses listed below may be subject to change from time to time.

National Fancy Rat Society (NFRS)
c/o Hon secr. Greg Baker
4 Salisbury Road, Ealing
London W13 9TX

NFRS, Membership coord.
c/o Elaine Johnston
4 Mayfair Court, Barn Hall Avenue
Colchester CO2 8TH

Swedish Rat Society (SRS)
c/o Potku Holmstedt
Kullstigen 10, 3tr
S-142 30 Trangsund
Sweden
(tel) 46-(0)8-7716718
or se homepage:
http://
www.stud.mdh.se/
~ltd92fsk/srs_
main.html

Finnish Rat Society
Eva-Lotte Mattsson
Ronnvagen 11
04130 SIBBO FINLAND
(tel) 90 231 867

American Fancy Rat and Mouse Assoc.
AFRMA Secretary
9230 64th Street
Riverside, CA 92509

Rat, Mouse & Hamster Fanciers
c/o John Langdell

1756 14th Ave.
San Francisco, CA 94122
(tel) (415) 564-6374

Mouse and Rat Breeders Assoc.
c/o Sharon Brown
127 Stockbridge Ln
Ojai, CA 93023
(tel) (805) 646-0663

The American Rat, Mouse and Hamster Society
c/o Sandy Ramey
9370 Adlai Road
Lakeside, CA 92040

Northeast Rat & Mouse International
c/o Diana Potter, Pres.
20 Oak Lane
Sterling, VA 20165
(tel) (703) 430-4063

Rat Fan Club
857 Lindo Lane
Chico, CA 95926
(tel) (916) 899-0605
debbie_ducommun@macgate.
csuchico.e du

Note from RFC president: If you send a self-addressed stamped envelope (SASE with international postage coupon from out of the U.S), I will send you a free introductory issue of the Rat Report and a list of back issues.

INDEX

A
Activity patterns, 28
Ammonia gas, 10
Anorexia, 38
Arthritis, 6
B
Barbering, 38
Bedding, 16
Behavior, 27
Berkshire, 10
Birth control, 35
Black rat, 4
Breeding Systems, 30
Brown rat, *see* Norway rat
C
Cages, 16
—Cleaning of, 18
Caries, 8
Chhromodacryorrhea, 39
Chronic murine pneumonia,
    44
Coat, 10
Coprophagy, 12
D
Defecation, 12
Diarrhea, 13
Diastema, 8
Diet, 24
Domestication, 6
E
Ears, 8
Environmental enrichment,
    21
Estrous cycle, 31
Euthanasia, 46
F
Face, 8
Feces, 12
Feeders, 17
Fostering, 35
G
Gait, 10
Gestation, 25, 32

Grooming, 13, 21
H
Hair chewing, *see* Barbering
Harderian gland, 39
Hearing, 12
Hooded rats, 10
Hybrid vigor, 15
I
Inbred strains, 15
K
Kidney failure, 44
L
Lactation, 25, 34
Life span, 6
Light, 20
Limbs, 9
Litters, 30
Lordosis, 32
M
Malocclusion, 37
Mating, 32
Mites, 46
N
Noise, 20
Norway rat, 4
O
Obesity, 24
Origin and spread, 4
Outbred stocks, 15
P
Parturition, 32
Pathogen-free rats, 15
Pheromones, 12
Pinworms, 45
Plague, 4
Pododermatitis, 37
Pregnancy, 32
Puberty, 30
Pups, 34
Q
Quarantine, 15
R
Rat bites, 22

Rat-baiting, 6
Rat-bite fever, 45
Ringtail, 36
Ringworm, 39
S
Salmonellosis, 45
Sex differentiation, 10
—in adults, 10
—in pups, 35
Sexual Maturity, 30
Shipping crates, 15
Shows, 29
Skeleton, 9
Slobbers, 38
Smell, 12
Superstitions, 3
Swimming, 21
T
Tail, 9
—injuries, 37
Taming, 6
Tapeworms, 45
Taste, 12
Teeth, 8
Temperature, 20
Thermoregulation, 13, 34
Touch, 11
Training, 28
Tumors, 41
U
Ulcerative dermatitis, 45
Urination, 12
V
Vaginal plug, 32
Ventilation, 18
Vibrissae, 11
Vision, 11
Vitamins, 24, 25
W
Water, 17, 24
Whelping, 32
Whiskers, *see* Vibrissae
Wild rat, 10